DISCARDED

DAUGHTER OF LIBERTY

A TRUE STORY OF THE AMERICAN REVOLUTION

Wyn Mabie's Route

New York
New Jersey
TAPPAN
WHITE PLAINS
OLD TAPPAN RD.
SCHRAALENBURG RD.
Hudson River
YONKERS
Westchester
HACKENSACK
FT. LEE RD.
FORT WASHINGTON
FORT LEE
WASHINGTON'S HEADQUARTERS
LONG ISLAND SOUND
HARLEM RIVER
New York Island
Hudson River
Long Island
QUEENS
NEW YORK CITY
EAST RIVER
KINGS (BROOKLYN)

DAUGHTER OF LIBERTY

A TRUE STORY OF THE AMERICAN REVOLUTION

Robert Quackenbush

Hyperion Books for Children
NEW YORK

For Margie and Piet

Printed in the United States of America.

First Edition
1 3 5 7 9 10 8 6 4 2

Artwork for this book was painted with gouache
on smooth Bristol paper.
Text for this book is set in 13-point Leawood Book.
Chapter headings are set in 36-point OPTI-Caslon Antique,
in the manner of the broadsides of the Revolutionary War.

Library of Congress Cataloging-in-Publication-Data
Quackenbush, Robert M.
Daughter of liberty / written and illustrated by Robert Quackenbush.
p. cm.
Summary: A chance encounter with General George Washington in upstate New York during the Revolutionary War leads a young woman to volunteer for a dangerous mission involving the retrieval of valuable papers.
ISBN 0-7868-1286-9 (trade: alk. paper)—ISBN 0-7868-2355-0 (library: alk. paper)
1. New York (State)—History—Revolution, 1775–1783—Juvenile fiction. [1. New York (State)—History—Revolution, 1775–1783—Fiction. 2. United States—History—Revolution, 1775–1783—Fiction.] I. Title.
PZ7.Q16 Dau 1998
[Fic]—dc21 98-12607

CONTENTS

There probably is no history,
only biography.
—Ralph Waldo Emerson, 1841

Chapter 1
Moonlight Ride

It was November 16, 1776. War had been raging on New York Island for three months. Twenty miles north of New York City, near the peaceful town of Tappan, Wyn Mabie galloped to her farm. She was late. She promised Aunt Susanna and the twins that she would be home before seven. Already a full moon was rising and the church bells were striking seven.

Wyn rode past Stone House, where

travelers often stopped for meals. The windows of the house were ablaze with candlelight.

Suddenly, a tall, caped figure appeared on the road.

"Stop, Hoost!" shouted Wyn, pulling hard on the reins.

Her horse skidded to a halt on a slanting, slippery bank and his hind legs slid from under him. Wyn seized his mane and he recovered just in time, narrowly missing the stranger.

"I'm sorry," came a man's voice from the shadows. "I didn't mean to frighten your horse."

The man stepped forth into the moonlight. He was wearing a long black cape with a high collar and a huge officer's hat.

"Oh!" said Wyn with surprise.

There before her stood General George Washington, commander in chief of the Continental Army.

Chapter 2

Chance Meeting

Wyn got down from Hoost.

"I am sorry for nearly running you down with my horse, General," she said. "My name is Wyn Mabie."

"How do you do," said Washington. "The fault was mine. I was deep in thought and I was not watching where I was going. No harm done. You are an excellent rider and I admire the ease and grace with which you regained control of your steed."

"Thank you, General," said Wyn. "I am fond of riding and Hoost and I work well together. We were just returning from an evening ride."

"I was having supper with some of my officers at Stone House," said Washington. Wyn knew that Stone House was a popular meeting place for patriots.

Washington continued, "After supper I decided to take a solitary stroll. My heart was heavy and my mind was filled with thoughts about what was discussed at the meeting. That is why I was not alert when you came down the road."

"Was Captain John Blauvelt at your meeting?" asked Wyn. "My husband, Abraham, is a private in his brigade at Stoney Point."

Wyn was anxious to hear any news of Abraham. She had not seen him since the middle of August when the British invaded New York.

"Yes, Captain Blauvelt was at the meeting," said Washington. "I recall seeing your husband's name on the roster."

"What is the news from the front lines?" asked Wyn.

"Not good, I regret to say," replied Washington. "This morning British forces captured Fort Washington, the last American stronghold on New York Island. I was with our troops in New Jersey when the fort was attacked. During the battle, I crossed the Hudson River from Fort Lee with one of my officers. I wanted to retrieve some papers from my headquarters at the Roger Morris House, an abandoned mansion near Fort Washington. The papers were hidden in my office. But we got there too late!"

"What happened?" asked Wyn.

Washington answered, "My officer and I watched from a nearby hillside as British soldiers stormed the mansion. We had to return to New Jersey without the papers. When Fort Washington fell, every American soldier was taken prisoner. The British Army now outnumbers the Continental Army three to one."

"How dreadful!" said Wyn. "What can we do?"

"More men and more supplies are needed, of course," said Washington. "The lost papers would help with that. They contain volunteer lists and letters of credit for supplies and weapons. We must put together a new set of papers. Valuable time will be lost doing it. In the meantime, my senior officers and I have sent out fresh appeals for men and supplies to representatives of each colony."

Wyn was silent for a moment.

At last she said, "Let me get the papers for you."

"Unthinkable," said Washington. "I lost one of my best officers on such a mission recently. He dressed as a schoolteacher and went to New York City to find out the next British moves. He was recognized and captured by British soldiers and hanged as a spy. His name . . ." Washington's voice quavered and he cleared his throat to continue. "His name was Nathan Hale."

"I know about Nathan Hale," said Wyn. "His inspiring last words have echoed through the colonies. He said that he regretted that he had only one life to lose for his country. I feel the same passion for America. You *must* let me go on this mission for you."

"It can't be done," said Washington. "The island is swarming with British troops."

"I could get through their lines," said Wyn. "The British would only stop a man. They do not bother with women and children."

"There is another problem," said Washington. "I have been informed that the British are reforming their troops and plan to invade New Jersey in two days, on November eighteenth."

"That gives me one day to get the papers," said Wyn. "I will be ready at dawn."

"It is too dangerous," said Washington.

"I am not afraid," said Wyn. "If you like, you may come home with me now to discuss it with my family. You'll meet my Aunt Susanna and my husband's ten-year-old twin cousins, Jan and Janneke. The twins' father, Reynier, is stationed with my husband at Stoney Point. Our farm is not far away and it will take only a few moments of your time. At least allow me this opportunity to show you some Dutch hospitality for almost running you down."

Washington smiled.

"Very well," he said. "I'll go with you to your farm. I'll leave from there for my headquarters in Hackensack. My carriage is nearby. Tie Hoost to the back of it and ride with me so we can talk on the way."

Chapter 3

War Game

The twins and Aunt Susanna were awestruck when Wyn opened the front door and walked in with General Washington.

Finally, Aunt Susanna managed to say, "Would you like some apple cider, General? It is freshly made, and very good."

"I would enjoy that very much," said Washington.

"I'll help you, Aunt Susanna," said Wyn.

Wyn and Aunt Susanna left the room.

Jan and Janneke sat on the floor in front of the fireplace, looking round-eyed in admiration at Washington. Spread out before them was a handmade map of the colonies. Placed on the map were cutout cardboard soldiers with blue coats and red coats.

"That is quite a display you have there," said Washington. "Did you make the map and the soldiers yourselves?"

The twins both nodded.

"What do you have your soldiers do?"

Jan and Janneke looked at each other to see who was to answer. Janneke pointed to Jan.

"It's a war game, General," said Jan. "We are pretending to fight America's War of Independence."

"Who is winning?" asked Washington.

"The Bluecoats," said Jan.

"I am certainly glad to hear that," said Washington. "I played war games myself when I was your age."

Janneke scowled and said, "Jan always has me be the Redcoats."

Just then Wyn and Aunt Susanna returned with cider and molasses cookies for everyone.

"General," said Aunt Susanna, "Wyn has been telling me how she wants to go to your headquarters in New York for papers you left behind. You had better let her go. Once she makes up her mind to do something, there is no stopping her. She has been like that since she was a child. Besides, she is the fastest rider in the county and you couldn't ask for a better messenger."

"You mean Wyn is going to be a messenger for General Washington?" said Jan, surprised.

Washington raised his hand. "I have not agreed to this," he said.

Jan turned to Wyn and said, "If you were to go, Wyn, how would you get there?"

"And how would you get back home?" asked Janneke.

"First I will go to Fort Lee by horseback," answered Wyn. "That is twelve miles south of here. There are boat docks at Fort Lee. I will row across the Hudson River to the northern banks of New York Island. Then I will find a way to get into General Washington's former headquarters and get the papers. That done, I will row back across the Hudson and deliver them to the new headquarters in Hackensack. The whole mission should take only a few hours. I will be home before dark."

Aunt Susanna smiled fondly at Wyn. Then she said to Washington, "You can see what I mean, General. Notice how Wyn says 'I will' be doing this and that. But what guarantee is there that the British have not already discovered your papers?"

"I hid them in a place where they would be difficult to find," said Washington. "And my headquarters was captured by the British only this morning. I doubt that the hiding place has been discovered in so short a time. Even so, such a perilous mission is out of the question."

Wyn spoke up. "I am not afraid. I *must* go, General. I owe it to my country and I owe it to my family. My husband and the twins' father are doing what they can. This is my chance to do something and I want to do it. The British must not win the war."

"What about your husband?" asked Washington. "What would he say?"

"He would say only one word," said Wyn. "He would say: *Go!*"

Everyone was silent for a moment.

Aunt Susanna said quietly, "I have faith that Wyn will succeed with this mission. Time is running out, General. You do not have many choices."

"And the twins?" said Washington. "What do you say?"

"We both say yes," said Jan and Janneke together.

"Then it's settled, General?" asked Wyn.

"It's settled," answered Washington. He reached into a pocket of his vest and pulled forth three pieces of paper. He handed Wyn the first piece of paper.

"Here is a pass with my signature to give to the guard at Fort Lee," said Washington. "He will help you get a rowboat. I will send word for him to expect you."

He unfolded the next piece of paper.

"This is a floor plan of the Roger Morris House," he said. "To get to the mansion you will have to cross Kingsbridge Road. Look for a stone bridge near the mansion. There is a path under the bridge that will get you to the other side of the road."

He pointed on the floor plan to the mansion's first floor.

Washington continued, "There are three entrances into the building: the main

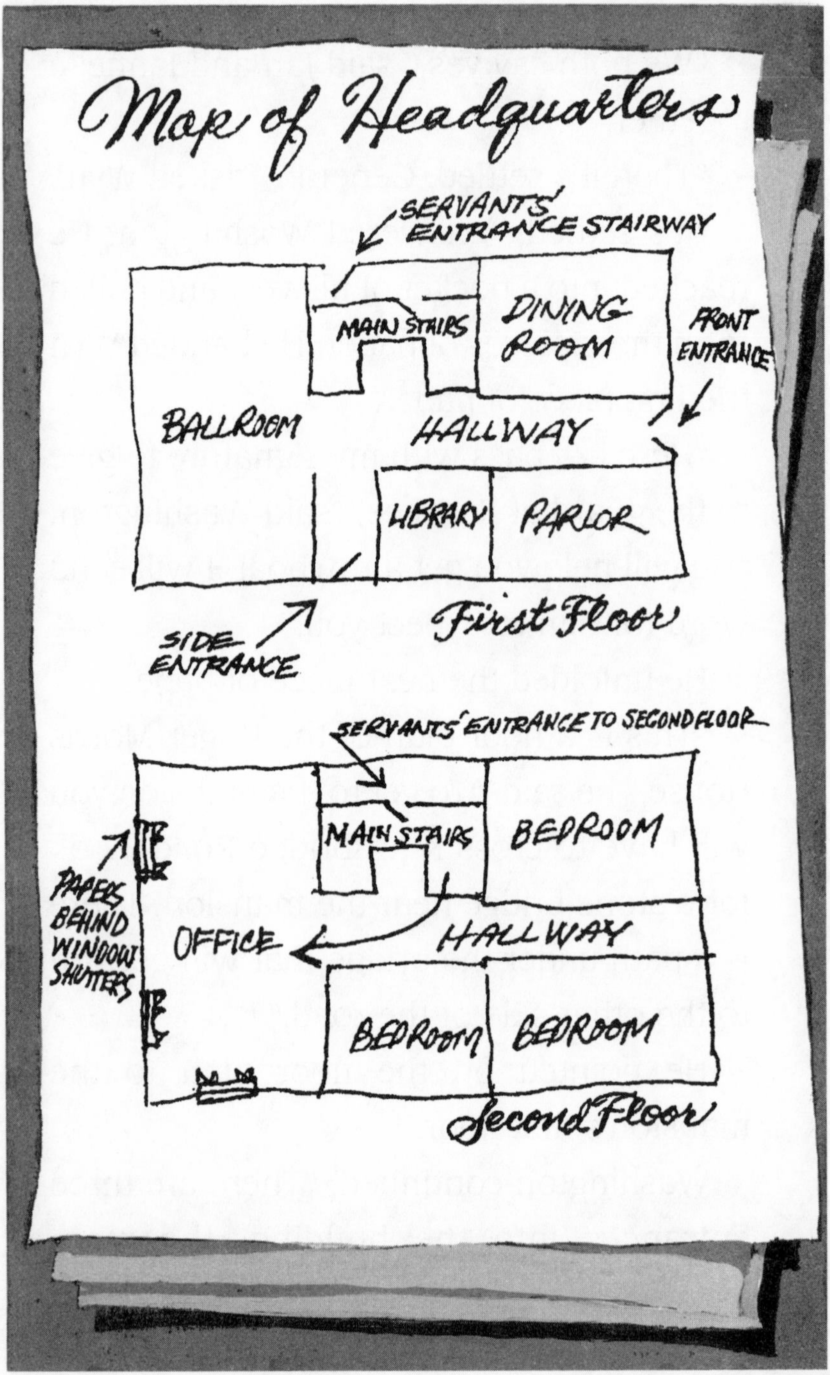

Map of Headquarters

SERVANTS' ENTRANCE STAIRWAY
MAIN STAIRS
DINING ROOM
FRONT ENTRANCE
BALLROOM
HALLWAY
LIBRARY
PARLOR
SIDE ENTRANCE
First Floor

SERVANTS' ENTRANCE TO SECOND FLOOR
MAIN STAIRS
BEDROOM
PAPERS BEHIND WINDOW SHUTTERS
OFFICE
HALLWAY
BEDROOM
BEDROOM
Second Floor

entrance, the side entrance, and the servants' entrance. The servants' entrance has a separate flight of stairs that leads to the second floor where I had my office."

Then he pointed on the floor plan to his office, on the mansion's second floor.

"When you enter the office you will see three windows," he said. "There are panels on the sides of each window. When these panels are opened, indoor window shutters unfold to cover the windows. The papers are hidden behind the shutters of the window to the far right as you enter the room."

He handed Wyn the floor plan and said, "When you are at the mansion, look for my housekeeper, Mrs. Thompson. She might still be there to help you. You will know her by her red hair. Whatever you do, be careful. Always remember that your life comes before the papers."

He handed Wyn the third piece of paper.

"Finally," he said, "here is a map to my headquarters in Hackensack. I will be awaiting your return. Good luck."

He got up and put on his cape. Wyn walked with him to the door. Pausing, he turned and looked back at the twins and their game. Then he said good-bye to everyone and walked out into the cold night air.

Chapter 4

Destiny's Ride

At dawn the next morning the twins and Aunt Susanna helped Wyn to prepare for her journey. Aunt Susanna packed Wyn's saddlebag with bread, cheese, apples, and a canteen filled with water. She brought it out to the barn where Wyn and the twins were putting a saddle and bridle on Hoost.

"It's cold, Wyn," Janneke said. "I've changed my mind. Maybe you should stay home."

"I know it's cold," said Wyn as she straightened the reins on Hoost. "But that doesn't bother me. Or Hoost. Isn't that true, Hoost? When we are out riding we don't think about cold weather. I am not worried about anything but winning right now."

"But why are you doing this?" asked Janneke.

Wyn answered, "I want my great-great-grandchildren to know that their great-great-grandmother went on a mission for General Washington during America's fight for independence."

"That's good enough reason for me," said Aunt Susanna. "Let's join hands in prayer before you go."

They all formed a circle and joined hands.

"Heavenly Father," said Aunt Susanna. "Touch the minds and hearts of all patriots wherever they may be and help to bring about true peace built on justice. Provide Wyn with a safe journey on her mission for General Washington. Amen."

"Amen," repeated Wyn and the twins.

Then Wyn climbed onto Hoost.

Janneke ran forward.

"I don't want you to go, Wyn," she cried. "I'm afraid. I don't want anything to happen to you. Please stay."

Wyn leaned in the saddle toward Janneke and said gently, "I'm not afraid, see, so why should you be afraid? Someday you will believe in something just as strongly as I believe in this mission."

With that, she rode away.

On the way to Fort Lee the wind was strong and cold. There were light snow flurries. Wyn searched the road ahead for every slippery spot or loose pebble that would cause Hoost to fall. What if he fell and she was injured? she thought. What would happen to her and Hoost? And who would get Washington's important papers in time?

She thought about Abraham, her husband. Had she seen him for the last time when he marched off to war from Tappan? She thought about Nathan Hale. Would she end up hanging from a tree like him?

She clenched her fists tight on the reins and shook off those terrible thoughts. "You can do it!" she shouted. "Think only of getting there!"

Determined and excited again, she urged Hoost faster.

Just then a horse and rider came tearing out of the woods. They were heading straight for Wyn and Hoost. The rider was bearded and wore a red scarf around his neck. He galloped alongside Wyn and Hoost. He reached over and snatched the reins from Wyn's hands.

"Give me your horse!" he snarled.

A horse thief! Wyn thought.

"Not on your life!" she shouted.

She grabbed the reins back and nudged Hoost with her heels to move faster. They raced ahead of the thief until they came to an open pasture. Wyn guided Hoost to make a quick turn, jump over a stone fence, and head across the pasture. She turned her head and saw the thief was far behind but still in hot pursuit of them. What can I do to get away from him? she thought.

Then she remembered that there was a small, abandoned church in the woods beyond the pasture. Perhaps she could hide there.

She came to a path that led through the woods and back to the road. The church was hidden among the trees off the path. She raced beyond the turnoff for the church to where the path met the road again. She pulled off her hair ribbon and threw it at the crossroads. Then she quickly guided Hoost to the turnoff.

When they got to the church, Wyn

brought Hoost to a halt. She jumped down and led him by the reins up the steps to the entrance. They were safe inside when they heard the thief coming down the path. They stood near a window where Wyn could keep watch.

"If anyone wants to know why we are here, Hoost," said Wyn, "I'll tell them that you wanted to be blessed. But don't relax too much. I don't want you to leave a mess on the floor. This is the Lord's house."

Wyn saw the thief race toward the crossroads. He stopped and picked up her ribbon. He looked to the right and then to the left of the main road. He scratched his head and then galloped away.

Wyn waited until she was sure it was safe to leave. Then she took Hoost by the reins and led him from the church to the crossroads. There was no one in sight.

"Good work, Hoost," said Wyn. "We got rid of the thief."

She reached in her saddlebag for an apple and gave it to Hoost. When he finished eating it, she climbed up on the saddle, urged Hoost with her heels to go right, and they headed down the road.

One hour later they arrived at the boat docks at Fort Lee. A guard from the Continental Army was expecting Wyn. She showed him the pass that Washington had given her.

The guard had stained yellow teeth and some of them were missing. His uniform was held together with pieces of rope. But to Wyn he was a welcome sight.

"I am glad to see you," she said. "Won't you have some bread and cheese with me?"

They ate silently together. Afterward, the guard helped her into a rowboat and took charge of Hoost. But before Wyn rowed away, he handed her a red ribbon.

"Attach this to your cloak, Miss," he said.

"It will help you when you get to British territory. The Tories—people who are loyal to the British—wear them."

"I refuse to wear it," said Wyn. "But thank you anyway."

"I admire your courage, Miss," said the guard. "Good luck."

Chapter 5

Across the River

The wind and snow flurries stopped, but the morning air was still cold as ice. The guard gave the rowboat a shove out into the water with his foot. Wyn picked up the oars and began to row. Her heart was pounding. Mist was forming on the water and she could barely see to the other side. It was a mile across. She figured it would take her an hour to row the distance.

As she rowed she felt blisters forming

through her thin, leather riding gloves. At midriver she paused and removed her gloves, and tore two pieces from the hem of her riding habit to wrap around her hands. Then she rowed all the harder.

"I will not give up! I will not give up!" she kept saying aloud.

Through the mist Wyn could see the banks of New York Island getting closer and closer. To the right she could see Harlem Heights. To the left was Fort Washington. In front of her was the Roger Morris House—Washington's headquarters—gleaming white on a hill.

At last Wyn got to the other side of the river. After she hid the boat in a bush, she climbed a rocky slope that led to the woods. She heard a commotion. She went peering from tree to tree until she saw what the noise was about. She had reached Kingsbridge Road.

Wyn was not prepared for what she saw.

Her eyes welled with tears. She saw half-naked American soldiers—many without shoes—being forced to march from Fort Washington to prison ships. The wounded were on wagons. They were bleeding, and many of them looked close to death.

Wyn burst into sobs.

"Pull yourself together!" she said aloud to herself. "You must do what you have to do—for them!"

She dried her eyes on her sleeve and proceeded through the woods along the edge of the road. She kept heading toward the mansion. At last she saw the stone bridge and the path that went under it. The path was next to a stream and was lined with trees and bushes. Wyn darted carefully from bush to bush. Then she tore along the path under the bridge to the other side.

I made it without being seen! she thought.

She saw the mansion ahead of her through the trees. It was ghostly white and it was framed by bare black trees that had lost all their leaves. The fallen leaves spread like a yellow blanket on the ground.

All was quiet. Too quiet. Wyn listened hard and heard the sound of voices and the clatter of dishes coming from inside the mansion.

Perfect! she thought. The enemy are having their noon meal. But how in the world am I going to get inside the mansion without Mrs. Thompson to help me?

Wyn looked around the grounds and at the windows of the house. Mrs. Thompson was nowhere in sight. Then Wyn saw a small cottage behind the mansion. She carefully worked her way over to it and peeked inside a window. No one was there. She saw a laundry basket on the floor and some clothes hanging on a line. She knew at once that this was a laundry cottage.

She got an idea. She opened the door of the cottage and went inside.

She reached down for the directions Washington had given her, which she had tucked into her boot. She studied the floor plan of the mansion. The servants' entrance was at the back of the mansion, away from the dining room where she heard the voices. She looked out a window and saw the same entrance. It was only fifty feet away. Then she glanced around the cottage. She saw a dress neatly folded on a table.

Just the thing! she thought as she held the dress up to her. *I'll disguise myself as one of the servants.*

She removed her hat and cape and pulled the dress over her riding habit. She finished off her disguise by fixing her hair in a chambermaid's bun on top of her head. Then she pulled some of the clothes off the line and stuffed them in the laundry basket.

When she was finished, she looked at her image in a broken mirror. She was satisfied that she resembled a laundry maid.

Wyn walked cautiously toward the mansion with the basket of clothes. She came to the servants' entrance and opened the door. She climbed the stairs that led to the main staircase of the mansion. Her temples were throbbing. She took a deep breath. Slowly she opened the door. No one was on the landing leading to the second floor where Washington's office was located.

She quickly and quietly climbed the main staircase to the second floor and turned right. Then she made her way down a narrow hall to the office. It was just as Washington had said it would be. She saw the window to the right of the room where he said his papers were hidden. But the panel to the right of the window was open! The shutters were pulled out of the recess!

Wyn felt like she had just received a blow to the stomach. Someone must have discovered the papers!

She ran to the window. She reached her hand into the recess and felt around inside. The papers were still there!

Wyn grabbed the papers and stuffed them in the same boot with Washington's instructions. As she turned to leave, she saw something on the desk in the center of the room. It was a paper file. She opened it and saw British plans for their next invasion. She saw where they were planning to set up a vast storehouse for food and weapons in Trenton, New Jersey. There was no time to look further at the file. She couldn't take the chance of being caught. She started to grab the file and take it with her.

Then she stopped herself. If the British found the file missing they might change their plans. Wyn would have to trust her memory.

She closed the file and headed back to

the servants' staircase carrying the laundry basket. Before she had time to get to the door she heard gruff voices coming from the hallway below. The British have finished their meal! thought Wyn. They are coming up the stairs!

Wyn pressed herself against the wall of the passageway. She slowly worked her way toward the door and reached for the knob. As she did, a floorboard squeaked. "Who's up there?" one of the voices called. Wyn heard the sound of heavy boots coming her way. Panicked, she ran down the servants' stairs and burst out the door.

Wyn hid in the woods next to the cottage. Three British officers came running from the mansion and began searching the grounds.

Suddenly, she heard a voice behind her.

"May I help you, dear?" someone was asking.

Startled, Wyn whirled around and saw the flaming red hair of Mrs. Thompson.

Chapter 6

Escape

Wyn explained to Mrs. Thompson who she was and why she was there.

"I will be glad to help you," said Mrs. Thompson. "It is a good thing you came for the papers today, because I will be leaving tonight. I have been allowed to rejoin my son and his family in Westchester."

Mrs. Thompson put her fingers to her lips. The British were very close by.

"Quick!" she whispered. "Give me the

laundry basket. Stay where you are. I'll take care of this."

She took the laundry basket and stepped out from the woods alone.

"What is it, gentlemen?" Wyn heard her say. "Are you looking for something?"

"Did you see someone leave the servant's entrance just now?" asked one of the officers. "We heard someone running down the stairs and out the door."

"That was me you heard," said Mrs. Thompson. "I was rushing to get some clothes from the laundry cottage."

The officers grumbled and went back to the house. Mrs. Thompson left with them. Just before she headed through the servant's entrance, she turned in Wyn's direction and smiled and nodded.

At that moment Wyn ducked into the laundry cottage and exchanged the maid's dress for her cape. Then she grabbed her hat and ran out the door of the cottage and headed for the stone bridge. She worked her way under the bridge, remembering all the horror that she had seen there. Wyn held her hand over her mouth to keep from crying out. She got past the bridge and looked over her shoulder. A British soldier was standing on the bridge waving wagons past. Did he see her? she wondered.

She ran as fast as she could and retraced her steps through the woods until she came to the bushes at the bottom of the hill where she had hidden the rowboat. Suddenly, she heard the sound of a musket being fired. She looked at the rocks above, but saw no one shooting.

She heard another shot and the zing of a bullet hitting a rock near her. Someone was shooting at her! She looked up and saw a British soldier. He stood on a high rock behind her. He was reloading his musket!

Wyn pushed the boat into the water and started rowing with all her might. Another

shot! This one narrowly missed her and hit the water.

She kept on rowing. At last she was out of range of the British soldier's musket. She paused to pick up the two pieces of cloth from the bottom of the boat that she had used to bind her hands on the way over. She wrapped her hands and continued pulling on the oars. Her arms were aching and her hands were bleeding through the cloth, but she would not stop rowing.

At last she could see the guard waiting for her at Fort Lee. Her eyes were focused only on him and watching his image grow bigger and bigger as she rowed closer and closer to him. When she reached her destination, the guard stepped into the water and pulled her rowboat to shore.

"You look like you had a bad time of it, Miss," he said. "Can I get you anything for your bleeding hands?"

"I'm fine," said Wyn with a huge sigh of

relief. "I have the papers. That's all that matters to me right now."

"I'll warn the troops to let you through," said the guard.

He hollered to a guard at the next station: *"Let the lady through! She is a messenger for General Washington! Pass the word along!"*

The call went echoing among the hills and valleys as Wyn galloped from Fort Lee to Hackensack. No one stopped her as she rode through the four thousand ragged American troops encamped there. Instead, soldiers on the road stood aside and cheered her all along the way.

Wyn found Washington waiting for her in front of his headquarters tent. She handed him the papers and told him what she had seen on the desk at the mansion about Trenton.

"I can't thank you enough for what you have done," said Washington. "I hope that we will meet again someday."

"I would be honored," said Wyn.

"In the meantime, I will have two of my best officers escort you back to Tappan," said Washington.

In good speed, Wyn arrived safely back home as promised, her mission accomplished.

Chapter 7

Homecoming

Wyn's mission was completed with no time to spare. The next day, eight thousand British troops crossed the Hudson River and captured Fort Lee. Washington and his meager army retreated to Pennsylvania. For the next several weeks the fighting stopped. When Christmas came, Abraham and Reynier were given leave to come home.

It was a joyful family reunion with presents

and good food to eat. Two days after Christmas, surprising news was brought to their door by their neighbor Johannes Meyer.

"Have you heard?" Johannes said. "On Christmas Day, General Washington and his troops made a surprise attack on a Hessian encampment at Trenton on the Delaware River. The Hessian soldiers were hired by the British to fight on their side. They were put in charge of a huge cache of food, weapons, and supplies at Trenton. They were not expecting the attack on Christmas morning. Washington took them prisoner and his prize was the British goods. This is a major blow to the British and will encourage more men to join Washington's army. I'm joining right away."

As Johannes rode off, the family gathered around Wyn. Jan and Janneke were jumping up and down.

"Did you hear that?" said Jan. "Wyn

helped General Washington to win a major victory!"

"Does the victory mean that the war will end soon?" asked Janneke.

"It will help," said Abraham. "It is the first turning point in favor of the Continental Army since the war started."

"Now people will have more faith that America can win the war," said Reynier. "Our army will increase in size and perhaps countries overseas will come to our aid."

Abraham put his arm around Wyn.

"I am so proud of you," he said.

"We are all proud of you," said Aunt Susanna.

"But there is one thing we should keep in mind," said Abraham. "We must keep our joy about what Wyn did a secret within the family. There are many Tories out there who might harm us if they knew that Wyn helped General Washington."

Wyn touched his arm.

"The twins know," she said. "I told them already that it is a family story—one for our great-great-grandchildren."

The following morning Aunt Susanna found two small packages placed in the twins' wooden shoes on the front doorstep. They were addressed to Jan and Janneke. She placed the packages at their places at the breakfast table.

"What is this?" cried Jan. "Another Christmas present?"

"A present for me?" cried Janneke.

They tore off the wrappings that covered two small boxes. Inside each box was a painted, metal Continental Army soldier. They were standing at attention, holding muskets at their sides.

"Who sent them?" asked Janneke.

"I have no idea," replied Aunt Susanna. "I found them in your wooden shoes on the front steps this morning. That is all I know."

"Look inside the boxes," said Wyn. "Perhaps you will find a note or a clue."

Jan and Janneke searched each box. There was no note, no sign of who had sent them.

"I wonder," said the twins together.

That evening when they went back to playing their war game, they included the new soldiers. The grown-ups sat around the fire watching them play.

"What are you doing on my side?" said Jan. "You are supposed to be a Redcoat. And I have just wiped you out at Trenton."

"You're wrong!" said Janneke. "I am a Bluecoat and I have this to prove it." She held up her metal soldier.

"I am a Bluecoat," she went on, "and I am proud of it. Bluecoats are brave, like Wyn. And Papa and Abraham, too. We Bluecoats are going to win this war for America's freedom and independence. I don't care how long it takes. We will win."

Then she turned to Wyn and asked, "Is that what you meant about someday believing strongly in something?"

"Definitely," said Wyn.

ABOUT THIS STORY

This story has evolved over many years of extensive research. It is a family account that was handed down to me from my father, his father, and his father's father—all the way back to Jacob Quackenbosch (*bosch* means bush in Dutch), father of Wyn Mabie. The events are all true. They were verified in genealogical records and historical records found in the Holland Society Library, the archives of Morris-Jumel Mansion, the New York Society Library, the

Genealogy Division of the New York Public Library, the New York Historical Society, and the Library of the Grand Lodge of the Masonic Temple of New York City.

The town of Tappan, in Rockland County, New York, is a well-known historical site from the days of America's Revolutionary War. Stone House—now called, "'76 House"—continues to be a popular place for travelers to dine. Another Tappan landmark is the DeWint House, where Washington established his headquarters in 1780. Research has shown that Wyn Mabie probably served once again as Washington's messenger when he had his headquarters at this location.

In New York City, Washington's headquarters at the Roger Morris House (now called Morris-Jumel Mansion) is also a well-known historical site. It is located at Roger Morris Park at West 160th Street and Edgecombe Avenue.

Just as Wyn Mabie intended, her story was passed down to her great-great-grandchildren. With this book, I am proud to have the opportunity to share her story for the inspiration and enjoyment of children everywhere.

—Robert Quackenbush
NEW YORK CITY
NOVEMBER 17, 1997

Enjoy More Hyperion Chapter Books!

ALISON'S PUPPY

SPY IN THE SKY

SOLO GIRL

MYSTERY OF
THE TOOTH GREMLIN

MY SISTER
THE SAUSAGE ROLL

I HATE MY BEST
FRIEND

ALISON'S FIERCE AND
UGLY HALLOWEEN

SECONDHAND STAR

GRACE THE PIRATE

Hyperion Chapters

2nd Grade

Alison's Fierce and Ugly Halloween
Alison's Puppy
Alison's Wings
The Banana Split from Outer Space
Edwin and Emily
Emily at School
The Peanut Butter Gang
Scaredy Dog
Sweets & Treats: Dessert Poems

2nd/3rd Grade

The Best, Worst Day
Grace's Letter to Lincoln
I Hate My Best Friend
Jenius: The Amazing Guinea Pig
Jennifer, Too
The Missing Fossil Mystery
Mystery of the Tooth Gremlin
No Copycats Allowed!
No Room for Francie
Pony Trouble
Princess Josie's Pets
Secondhand Star
Solo Girl
Spoiled Rotten

3rd Grade

Behind the Couch
Christopher Davis's Best Year Yet
Daughter of Liberty
Eat!
Grace the Pirate
Koi's Python
The Kwanzaa Contest
The Lighthouse Mermaid
Mamá's Birthday Surprise
My Sister the Sausage Roll
Racetrack Robbery
Secret Pal Surprises
Spy in the Sky
Third Grade Bullies